Rachel Carson:

Renowned Marine Biologist and Environmentalist

by Gina Dal Fuoco

Science Contributor
Sally Ride Science

Science Consultants
Nancy McKeown, Planetary Geologist
William B. Rice, Engineering Geologist

MISSION: SCIENCE

Developed with contributions from Sally Ride Science™

Sally Ride Science™ is an innovative content company dedicated to fueling young people's interests in science.

Our publications and programs provide opportunities for students and teachers to explore the captivating world of science—from astrobiology to zoology.

We bring science to life and show young people that science is creative, collaborative, fascinating, and fun.

To learn more, visit www.SallyRideScience.com

First hardcover edition published in 2009 by
Compass Point Books
151 Good Counsel Drive
P.O. Box 669
Mankato, MN 56002-0669

Editor: Jennifer VanVoorst
Designer: Heidi Thompson
Editorial Contributor: Sue Vander Hook

Art Director: LuAnn Ascheman-Adams
Creative Director: Joe Ewest
Editorial Director: Nick Healy
Managing Editor: Catherine Neitge

 This book was manufactured with paper containing at least 10 percent post-consumer waste.

Library of Congress Cataloging-in-Publication Data
Fuoco, Gina Dal.
 Rachel Carson : renowned marine biologist and environmentalist / by Gina Dal Fuoco.
 p. cm. — (Mission: Science)
 Includes index.
 ISBN 978-0-7565-4074-6 (library binding)
1. Carson, Rachel, 1907–1964—Juvenile literature. 2. Biologists—United States—Biography—
Juvenile literature. 3. Environmentalists—United States—Biography—Juvenile literature.
I. Title.
 QH31.C33F86 2009
 570.92—dc22
 [B]   2008037625

Visit Compass Point Books on the Internet at *www.compasspointbooks.com*
or e-mail your request to *custserv@compasspointbooks.com*

Table of Contents

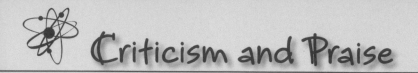

Rachel Carson expected people to criticize her latest book. She even braced herself for possible lawsuits by some of the largest chemical companies in the world. Exposing the dangers of pesticides would certainly affect business. And the companies didn't believe their pesticides were hurting anything but harmful insects and weeds.

Carson didn't agree. In fact, she believed that a pesticide called DDT was harming birds and other animals—perhaps even humans. She had the support of scientists who had already studied her book chapter by chapter. They had come to the same conclusion: Spraying DDT on farm crops was damaging the environment.

When *Silent Spring* was published in 1962, Carson received all the criticism she expected. But others praised her work—and her courage. This quiet nature lover and writer would spark an international uproar that would transform how the world looked at the environment and the way it used chemicals.

Rachel Carson

Changing Our Ideas About Nature

The first signs of damage to the environment often show up in ocean life. Scientists study sea life to understand what may be happening on the entire planet.

Rachel Carson wanted people to understand how humans are just one link in the chain of nature. When we damage one link, we alter the entire chain. We are all part of a food web, and each part is closely tied to the others. When part of the web changes, the other parts are affected and become unbalanced. For example, when there are too many seals in an ecosystem, there won't be enough squid for them to eat. Many seals will starve and die. Fewer seals means less food for sharks, which will cause the shark population to decline. When there are fewer sharks, the seal population will rise again.

Humans are also part of the food web. Our actions affect our food sources. A healthy Earth depends on harmony among all the food webs. Everything is connected: What one species does affects all the other species. Humans have the responsibility to protect and preserve other living things.

Sea lions, a kind of eared seal, are part of a complex food web that involves many other marine plants and animals.

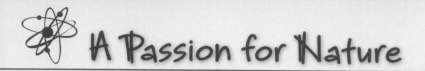

Rachel Carson was born May 27, 1907, the third and last child of Robert and Maria Carson. Her family lived on a 65-acre (26-hectare) farm near Springdale, Pennsylvania, along the Allegheny River.

Rachel spent hours exploring the outdoors. Ponds, streams, forests, and meadows were her playground. Flowers, birds, and other animals captured her interest day after day. Sometimes she just sat and looked at the beautiful world around her. The outdoors was also a sort of classroom. There Rachel's mother taught her children all she knew about the natural world. From her mother, Rachel acquired a lifelong passion for nature. The ocean would come to fascinate her the most.

Rachel enjoyed reading and writing from a very young age. At the age of 8, she decided she would be an author. Her first tales were about animals. When she was 10, her story "A Battle in the Clouds" was published in a children's magazine.

▼ The Allegheny River flows near Carson's childhood home in Springdale, Pennsylvania.

From early childhood the ocean filled Rachel Carson with a sense of wonder.

In 1925, 18-year-old Rachel Carson graduated from high school at the top of her class. The following year she attended Pennsylvania College for Women (now Chatham University) to study English. But a required biology class sparked her interest in science. She changed her major.

In 1929, Carson graduated from college with honors, with a degree in biology. That summer she studied at the Marine Biological Laboratory in Woods Hole, Massachusetts. Three years later she received her master's degree in zoology from Johns Hopkins University in Baltimore, Maryland. It was a remarkable accomplishment at that time for a woman to graduate from college. It was also rare for a woman to become a scientist. Most women who did attend college studied how to become better homemakers.

Although Carson had planned to get a doctoral

▲ Young Rachel Carlson

degree, she had to get a full-time job instead. Her parents were having financial difficulties and needed her help. When her father died unexpectedly in 1935, her mother needed her even more. Carson moved in with her to support her completely.

Carson got a job with the U.S. Bureau of Fisheries as a marine biologist. But in 1937, Carson's only sister died. Now Carson took on the responsibility of raising her sister's two daughters.

Marine Biology

As a marine biologist, Carson studied the animals and plants of the sea, as well as life along the shore. Marine biologists study a huge variety of marine animals, researching their habitats, their food, and their behaviors.

The formal study of sea life began in the late 1800s when groups of biology students began spending their summers investigating the seashores in the United States and Europe. In 1888, the Marine Biological Laboratory opened in Woods Hole, Massachusetts. Although it started out as a school for beginning zoology students and teachers, the director soon expanded the opportunities. Advanced courses in marine biology attracted more serious students. By the time Carson attended in the summer of 1929, the school was accepting only advanced students and researchers.

Marine biologists in the field tag a loggerhead turtle in order to track its movement.

Rachel Carson was fortunate to have a good job so she could support her mother and two nieces. Her duties at the U.S. Bureau of Fisheries included studying sea life and writing the script for a weekly radio program called "Romance Under the Waters." The job was a perfect fit—a mixture of zoology and writing. She was captivated by the ocean and its great variety of life. She enjoyed telling people about the spectacular sea that teemed with colorful fish and plants. Most people at that time didn't know much about the mysterious underwater world.

Eventually Carson was promoted to editor-in-chief of all publications. In her spare time she wrote articles for magazines and newspapers. "Undersea," a vivid description of the ocean, was a popular piece. In 1941, it was published as a book titled *Under the Sea Wind*.

Carson was already working on another book, *The Sea Around Us*. Before it was published, magazines were printing some of the chapters, and *Reader's Digest* published a condensed version. The best-selling book received two awards and was made into a film.

Carson had an exceptional ability to write about nature in vivid, interesting prose. In 1952, she was awarded two honorary doctorates. It was a high honor to be given a doctoral degree without going through the normal college course work. She also made a big change in her life that year: She quit her government job and became a full-time writer.

A Writing Life

Carson recalled, "I can remember no time, even in earliest childhood, when I didn't assume I was going to be a writer. Also, I can remember no time when I wasn't interested in the out-of-doors and the whole world of nature. Those interests, I know, I inherited from my mother and have always shared with her."

A Way With Words

Carson's book *The Sea Around Us* was eventually published in 32 languages. A documentary film based on the book won the 1953 Oscar for Best Documentary. However, Carson wasn't happy with the script and never again allowed one of her books to be made into a film.

Did You Know?

The U.S. Bureau of Fisheries (later called the U.S. Fish and Wildlife Service) was created in 1940. The agency is part of the U.S. Department of the Interior, a government agency developed to preserve and protect wildlife. The service now has more than 40,000 volunteers. Together they do more than a million hours of work each year.

Rachel Carson was not only a best-selling author; she was also a popular speaker. Letters poured in from enthusiastic readers. Invitations came from all over the country for her to speak about her books and share the wonders of the ocean. With ample income from her books, Carson could devote more time to what she enjoyed most—writing. She wrote more books and magazine articles. She even wrote a script for an educational television program.

Helping people understand nature was rewarding to Carson. She wanted people to experience and appreciate the beauty and wonder of Earth's vast resources. But Carson also wanted her readers to realize that humans have the power to damage the planet. And once Earth is harmed, it may not be able to be repaired.

Carson encouraged people to care for their planet. She explained that humans are only one part of nature— the part that has the power to damage it. It wasn't long before she realized that real damage was indeed being done to Earth. She especially took note of a synthetic pesticide called DDT.

A farmer sprays pesticides ➡ on his crop of flowers.

Pests and Pesticides

Certain insects and weeds can harm or destroy farm crops. Farmers use pesticides to kill these harmful pests. Pesticides help farmers grow more crops with less damage or loss. But pesticides sometimes harm more than unwanted pests. They can damage other living things, including animals and people. The chemicals in synthetic pesticides remain in the soil for many years. Rain often washes chemicals into ponds, streams, or oceans. Pesticides can also get into vegetables or grains that people eat and seep into the water that people drink. People and animals also breathe in airborne pesticides, which are transported by the wind to various places.

Some people are turning to organic foods, which have not been sprayed with pesticides. Standards that organic farmers have to meet make the food they produce healthier. The demand for organic foods grows each year.

↑ international symbol for biohazards and poisons

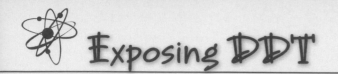

During World War II, DDT was used to kill mosquitoes to control malaria and other mosquito-borne diseases. Sometimes entire cities were sprayed with the chemical to kill mosquitoes or lice that were spreading typhus. By the end of the war in 1945, this so-called "insect bomb" was very popular all over the world. More and more uses for DDT were being found.

In 1955, the World Health Organization, an agency of the United Nations, developed a program to completely rid the world of malaria by spraying DDT. The program received high praise, and malaria was indeed eliminated in some areas of the world.

Widespread spraying of farm crops as well as surrounding land got under way in 1957. Airplanes carrying DDT—"crop dusters" as they were called—regularly swooped down on farmland, leaving enormous plumes of the chemical that eventually settled to the ground. DDT was one of the most effective pesticides farmers had ever used.

Rachel Carson was aware of the extensive use of DDT, and she watched the effects it was having on wildlife. After all, she argued, if the powerful chemical could kill a variety of pests, it could also damage or destroy other animals, and even humans. Other scientists were also concerned, but their concerns received little attention.

Did You Know?

By the late 1960s, many mosquitoes had developed a natural resistance to DDT. Over time, they had adapted to the chemical, which no longer destroyed them. Today more than 500 insects and 270 weeds are resistant to one or more pesticides.

DDT

DDT is not a natural substance. It is a synthetic chemical that was first produced in a laboratory in 1874. In 1939, Swiss scientist Paul Müller discovered that DDT killed insects. It proved to be valuable, especially for eradicating insects that spread diseases. Later farmers valued it highly for its ability to get rid of the insects and weeds that constantly threatened to destroy their crops.

DDT was powerful, effective, and long-lasting. It stayed in the soil and water, and remained in plant and animal tissue for many years. DDT was given partial credit for doing away with malaria in North America and Europe. So significant was this pesticide that Müller was awarded the 1948 Nobel Prize in physiology and medicine for his work with DDT.

▲ Wheat is sprayed with DDT.

▲ Insect pests eat the DDT. Most die, but not right away.

▲ Birds eat the insects and are poisoned by the DDT.

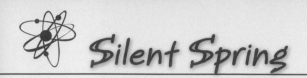

The world was excited about the benefits of DDT, but not everyone praised the pesticide. In 1957, the editor of *The New York Times* asked Rachel Carson to write an article on the dangers of DDT. Carson was in the middle of another family tragedy. Earlier in the year, one of her nieces she had raised died at the age of 31. She left behind a 5-year-old son named Roger. Again Carson took on the responsibility of raising an orphaned child and adopted the boy. She was also still caring for her aging mother. But despite her family responsibilities, Carson found time to take on *The New York Times'* challenge.

Carson had been studying the effects of DDT for years—especially what the chemical was doing to birds. Off the coast of Cape Cod, Massachusetts, birds were dying at an alarming rate. Carson also noticed that their eggshells were becoming thinner, resulting in problems or death for baby birds. She claimed that DDT was a danger to the whole environment—plants, animals, and humans.

The article grew into a book called *Silent Spring*, which was published in 1962. It took Carson four years to write her detailed description of the effects of DDT. While most pesticides killed one or two types of

"A Fable for Tomorrow"

The most famous chapter of *Silent Spring* was "A Fable for Tomorrow." In it Carson described a make-believe American town where there was no more new life—no baby birds, no young fish, no human children, no new blossoms on the trees. Springtime was silent in this town affected by DDT.

Protecting the Birds

Rachel Carson wasn't the first person to be concerned about birds. In 1930, environmentalist Rosalie Barrow Edge (1877–1962) challenged the Audubon Society for allowing hunting in the Rainey Wildlife Sanctuary in Louisiana. The sanctuary was supposed to be an area where wildlife was protected. Because of Edge's efforts, hunting ended there in 1934.

In the meantime, Edge was establishing a wildlife preserve of her own. Hawk Mountain in eastern Pennsylvania was a regular stop for hawks on their migration route. But hunters were shooting the hawks for sport. Edge raised $3,500, purchased the mountaintop land, and created the Hawk Mountain Sanctuary. Visitors from around the world visit this sanctuary where hunting is forbidden. People come especially in the fall when the largest groups of eagles, hawks, and falcons soar freely.

insects, DDT could destroy hundreds of varieties at once. It was killing the bad as well as the good insects. DDT remained toxic for weeks or months after it was sprayed. Even rainwater didn't weaken the hardy pesticide. Carson warned that DDT had already harmed birds and other animals, and as a result it had harmed everything in the food web.

Carson explained in her book how the chemical stayed in the fatty tissues of animals and humans and could cause cancer. She believed that DDT could destroy entire species. Then she bravely attacked some of the largest chemical companies in the world. She accused them of spreading false information about the pesticide. And she blamed government officials for not questioning what the companies claimed.

Carson at the time *Silent Spring* was published ⬆

When *Silent Spring* was written, Europe had already banned the use of mercury oxide to cover seeds. It took Carson's book ⬇ to get the United States to do the same.

Ecosystems

Rachel Carson introduced the word *ecosystem* in her book *Silent Spring*. An ecosystem is a community of living things and the environment in which they live. All living things in an ecosystem work together and depend on each other.

The title of Carson's book was significant. She believed that if people continued to use DDT, springtime would one day be silent—no bees buzzing, no birds chirping, and no frogs croaking. Carson's book immediately caused an uproar. It frightened readers around the world and enraged the chemical industry and farmers. This quiet scientist and popular writer found herself in the middle of a worldwide controversy. Some people condemned her, and others praised her for exposing the harmful effects of DDT. Carson's book had lit the fire of the environmental movement in the United States.

In a silent spring, the sounds of the natural world would be absent because the creatures who made the noises would have been destroyed.

The chemical companies fought back. They claimed that Carson's ideas would return society to the Dark Ages when insects spread a variety of diseases. One company published a pamphlet titled "The Desolate Year" that described a world where banned pesticides brought about uncontrolled diseases and insects.

Carson wasn't surprised at the reaction to her book. In fact, she had expected it. Before *Silent Spring* was published, a long list of leading scientists had read the book and warned her of the criticism she would receive. But they agreed with what Carson wrote. Now those same scientists supported her. And some people began to understand that if humans harmed the natural world, they were also harming themselves.

Did You Know?

Rachel Carson was named one of *Time* magazine's 100 most influential people of the 20th century.

The Audubon Society

With the help of the Audubon Society, Rachel Carson reached more people with information about the harmful effects of DDT. Founded in 1905, the Audubon Society boasted 39,000 members in its first year. Members signed a pledge to not mistreat birds. The environmental organization, named after naturalist John James Audubon, is one of the oldest organizations in the world. Its mission is to educate the public about birds and preserve and restore birds and their habitats.

Silent Spring caused quite a commotion in the United States. Rachel Carson received hundreds of invitations to speak to groups and on television. On April 3, 1963, she was featured on *CBS Reports.* To an audience of millions, she read parts of her book and met her critics face to face. Support grew for Carson, and the environmental movement became stronger.

After reading *Silent Spring*, President John F. Kennedy ordered the Science Advisory Committee to examine the effects of DDT. Carson testified before committee members, who later reported that Carson's claims were true. The committee recommended that DDT and other toxic pesticides be phased out. The government began tightening regulations on this now-controversial pesticide.

Friend of the Everglades

Journalist Marjory Stoneman Douglas (1890–1998) often wrote about environmental issues. Her book, *The Everglades: River of Grass,* described the Florida Everglades, an area she spent her life trying to protect. At one time, the Everglades were considered a useless swamp. Areas were drained and filled in with dirt to develop the land for homes and businesses. In 1969, when she was 79 years old, Douglas formed Friends of the Everglades to stop an airport from being built in the Everglades. She was awarded a Presidential Medal of Freedom, and her grassroots organization continues to protect and restore the Florida Everglades.

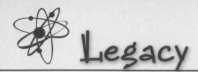

In 1972, the United States banned the use of DDT. In the meantime, individuals and scientists had started paying more attention to the environment. People were noticing polluted water, dirty air, and dying animals. Groups started working toward a common cause—a cleaner environment.

Rachel Carson didn't live to celebrate the ban of DDT in the United States. She died from cancer on April 14, 1964, at the age of 56. But she would be remembered as one of the most significant people of the century. Her quiet life and sensitive writing would inspire an entire generation to take a closer look at the environment and take action to preserve it.

The impact of Carson's life didn't end when she died. In fact, it grew into a nationwide environmental movement and led to the creation of the Environmental Protection Agency in 1970. The agency's main goal is to protect human health and preserve the natural environment.

In 1980, 16 years after her death, Rachel Carson was awarded the Presidential Medal of Freedom for her role in founding the environmental movement. The medal is the highest honor a U.S. civilian can receive from the government.

Landmarks

Carson's childhood home in Springdale, Pennsylvania, called the Rachel Carson Homestead, is on the National Register of Historic Places. Her home in Colesville, Maryland, where she wrote *Silent Spring,* was designated a National Historic Landmark in 1991. The Rachel Carson Bridge in Pittsburgh and the Pennsylvania Department of Environmental Protection building are both named in her honor.

The Green Belt Movement

Like Rachel Carson, Wangari Maathai is an environmentalist. Born in 1940 in Kenya, Africa, Maathai received two college degrees in the United States and a doctorate in Kenya.

In 1986, Maathai founded the Green Belt movement, an organization in Kenya that restores trees where forests have been cut down or burned. For every 100 trees destroyed, only nine were being replanted. Deforestation was destroying animals' natural habitats and limiting firewood that people needed to warm their homes. Without the natural balance of tree life, even the water was becoming polluted.

The Green Belt movement hires women from villages in Kenya to plant trees. The organization benefits the environment as well as Kenyan families. In 2004, Maathai won the Nobel Peace Prize for her work.

Still Around

DDT has not been used in the United States since 1972. But a scientist recently found high levels of the pesticide in songbirds that live in the United States.

Other people besides Rachel Carson have believed deeply in preserving our environment. Many of them were also influential writers and established environmental organizations that are still active today.

John Muir (1838–1914) founded the Sierra Club in 1892 to preserve the Sierra Nevada mountains in California. Today the club has nearly a million members who work together to explore, enjoy, and protect the wilderness areas of our planet. Each year the club takes groups on outings to learn about and appreciate the beauty of nature.

▲ John Muir

The World Wildlife Fund was established in 1961 to protect nature. Members work in countries all over the world to protect habitats and maintain a healthy life for all living things. They work to preserve rain forests, coral reefs, endangered species, and natural resources.

The mission of Greenpeace, founded in 1971, is to protect and conserve the environment and promote peace. Members seek to expose problems such as over-fishing and the dangers of nuclear energy.

The work of Rachel Carson continues today through the work of these and other environmental organizations. Individuals can also carry on what Carson and others began. Every person can be an environmentalist by recycling cans, plastic, and

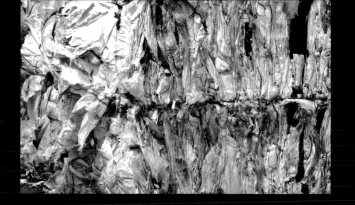

Americans throw away enough paper each year to build a wall 12 feet (3.6 meters) high, stretching from Los Angeles to New York City.

more. We can use things over and over instead of throwing them away. Or we can give our used items to others who may need them. And finally, we can cut down on the resources we use. By turning off a light or riding your bicycle instead of driving a car, you are protecting the environment and preserving its natural resources.

Together we can keep Rachel Carson's dream alive. We can share in her wonder of nature and work to protect it for the future.

Where Have All the Frogs Gone?

Through the years, many species have become extinct—some by natural causes and others because of human damage to the environment. Natural events caused dinosaurs to disappear from Earth. But scientists are now concerned about animals such as the brightly colored harlequin frog. Scientists are trying to figure out why so many of them are dying. Some think it's a combination of climate change and a harmful fungus. Perhaps there are changes we can make to our environment to save species from extinction.

Marine Biologist: Sylvia Earle

Deep Ocean Engineering

Sylvia Earle is an exceptional marine biologist. She has walked on the sea floor deeper than any other human. To make her deep dive, she used special diving gear called a JIM suit.

Earle has spent her entire career exploring and studying the ocean. Her research is done mostly underwater in submarines and submersibles that go where no human has gone before.

Earle wants to be remembered as someone who cares. In fact, she cares so much that she stopped eating seafood. "I know too many fish personally," she quipped.

▼ Earle shows a specimen to another scientist inside a research submarine.

▲ Earle prepares for a deep
dive in a special JIM suit.

Earle is also an environmentalist
who wants to protect all living
things in the sea. She has even
given advice to presidents about
how to care for our oceans.
Like Rachel Carson, Earle
is a writer with numerous
publications and books.

In 1992, Earle and her husband,
Graham Hawkes, founded
Deep Ocean Engineering.
Their California-based business
designs and operates submarine
systems—some piloted and
others robotic—that operate at
extreme ocean depths.

Lots of Life

Sylvia Earle recalled, "What
really captured my attention
as a kid is the enormous
variety of life in the ocean."

Think About It

As a girl, Earle loved playing
with horseshoe crabs on
the beach even though
they looked scary. She says
scientists need to be curious.
What are you curious about?

29

Name:	Rachel Carson
Date of birth:	May 27, 1907
Nationality:	American
Birthplace:	Springdale, Pennsylvania
Parents:	Robert and Maria Carson
Children:	Roger Christie (adopted, niece's son)
Field of study:	Marine biology, writer
Known as:	Mother of the environmental movement
Contributions to science:	Environmental awareness
Awards and honors:	Presidential Medal of Freedom (awarded posthumously in 1980)
Publications:	*Under the Sea Wind*, 1941 *The Sea Around Us*, 1951 *The Edge of the Sea*, 1955 *Silent Spring*, 1962

Barry Commoner (1917–   )
American biologist, educator, and environmental activist; outlined the four laws of ecology in his 1971 book, *The Closing Circle*

Paul Ralph Ehrlich (1932–   )
American biologist and educator who first proposed the theory that human survival depends on the realization that Earth's natural resources are nonrenewable and too limited to support the growing population; wrote *The Population Bomb* in 1968

Charles Sutherland Elton (1900–1991)
British environmental scientist who developed in the 1920s the idea that organisms form a pyramid of food levels that keep the energy flow within the ecosystem in balance; at the base are the producers and at the top are herbivores and a small number of carnivores

Aldo Leopold (1886–1948)
American naturalist who was one of the first scientists to arouse public interest in wilderness conservation; wrote *A Sand Country Almanac*

Robert Helmer MacArthur (1930–1972)
American environmental scientist who, along with Edward O. Wilson, wrote *The Theory of Island Biogeography,* which marked the beginning of biogeography, a branch of environmental science that focuses on stable ecological systems

Thomas Robert Malthus (1766–1834)
British economist who wrote some of the earliest accounts of problems encountered by an expanding human population

George Perkins Marsh (1801–1882)
American statesman, diplomat, and scholar who is
noted for his pioneering work in the field of conservation

John Muir (1838–1914)
British-born American naturalist who is noted for his work
to gain popular and federal support of forest conservation

Paul Hermann Müller (1899–1965)
Swiss chemist who discovered the effect of the
insecticide DDT; won the Nobel Prize in 1948

Gifford Pinchot (1865–1946)
American public official who made several great
conservation contributions during Theodore Roosevelt's
presidency (1901–1909)

John Wesley Powell (1834–1902)
American geologist, ethnologist, and anthropologist
whose explorations of the United States, especially in
the West, laid the groundwork for numerous federal
conservation projects

Gilbert White (1720–1793)
British naturalist who wrote *The Natural History and
Antiquities of Selborne,* one of the first known works
on ecology

Edward Osborne Wilson (1929–   )
American entomologist, ecologist, and sociobiologist
who, along with Robert H. MacArthur, wrote *The
Theory of Island Biogeography,* which marked the
beginning of biogeography, a branch of ecology
that focuses on stable ecological systems

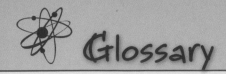

biology—science of living organisms

civil service—government work; employment usually is on the basis of competitive exams

crop dusters—airplanes used for spreading chemicals such as pesticides from above

DDT—chemical pesticide that is also harmful to animals and humans; used extensively in the 1940s and 1950s and banned in 1972

deforestation—cutting down or destruction of forests

doctorate—highest advanced degree earned by study and research at a college or university

ecosystem—community of living organisms and their environment and how they interact and depend on each other to survive

environment—natural world of land, sea, air, plants, and animals

Everglades—swampy region of southern Florida; a portion of the region makes up Everglades National Park

extinct—no longer existing

food web—multiple food chains connected within an ecosystem

habitat—where plants or animals live in their natural states

malaria—disease characterized by periodic attacks of chills and fever that is transmitted by the bite of certain mosquitoes

marine biology—science of life and living organisms in the sea and how they function and grow

migration—periodic movement of an animal from one region or climate to another for feeding or breeding

natural resources—any substance found in nature that people use, such as soil, air, trees, coal, and oil

organic—produced without the use of chemically formulated fertilizers, growth stimulants, antibiotics, or pesticides

pesticide—substance, usually chemical, applied to crops to kill harmful insects and other creatures

preserve—keep in unchanged condition; protect from harm

recycle—reprocess and reuse old material into a new use or function

resistant—able to withstand the effects of harmful environmental agents such as pesticides

sanctuary—refuge for wildlife where predators are controlled and hunting is illegal

synthetic—artificial or manufactured

toxic—capable of causing injury or death, especially by chemical means

typhus—disease marked by fever, confusion, headache, and rash; transmitted especially by body lice

zoology—scientific study of animals

1907	Born May 27 near Springdale, Pennsylvania
1915	Decides she will become a writer; begins writing about animals
1917	At the age of 10 writes "A Battle in the Clouds," which is published in a children's magazine
1925	Graduates from high school at the top of her class; enrolls in Pennsylvania College for Women to study English; later changes her major to biology
1929	Graduates from college with honors; studies for the summer at the Marine Biological Laboratory in Woods Hole, Massachusetts
1932	Receives a master's degree in zoology from Johns Hopkins University in Baltimore, Maryland
1935	Her father dies; lives with and supports her mother
1936	Hired full time by the U.S. Bureau of Fisheries as a marine biologist
1937	Her only sister dies; takes the responsibility of raising her sister's two daughters
1941	Her first book, *Under the Sea Wind*, is published
1945	Use of the pesticide DDT begins worldwide to destroy disease-bearing insects
1951	*The Sea Around Us* is published; becomes a best seller

1952	Awarded two honorary doctoral degrees
1955	World Health Organization develops a program to completely rid the world of malaria by spraying DDT
1957	Widespread spraying of farm crops with DDT gets under way; crop dusters regularly spray the pesticide on farmland; Carson writes articles for *The New York Times* on the dangers of DDT
1962	*Silent Spring* is published and receives mixed reactions
1963	Featured on television program *CBS Reports;* receives numerous invitations to speak about her book *Silent Spring;* President Kennedy reads her book and orders the Science Advisory Committee to examine the effects of DDT
1964	Dies of cancer April 14
1970	Environmental Protection Agency is created to protect human health and preserve the natural environment
1972	The United States bans the use of DDT
1980	Awarded the Presidential Medal of Freedom posthumously (after her death)

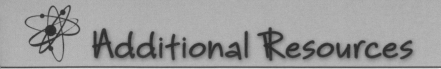

Carson, Rachel. *The Sea Around Us*. New York: Oxford University Press, 2003.

Carson, Rachel. *Silent Spring*. Boston: Houghton Mifflin, 2002.

Donald, Rhonda Lucas. *Water Pollution*. New York: Children's Press, 2001.

Macfarlane, Katherine. *Pesticides*. Detroit: KidHaven Press, 2007.

Spilsbury, Louise. *Environment at Risk: The Effects of Pollution*. Chicago: Raintree, 2006.

Stille, Darlene R. *Nature Interrupted: The Science of Environmental Chain Reactions*. Minneapolis: Compass Point Books, 2008.

On the Web

For more information on this topic, use FactHound.

1. Go to *www.facthound.com*
2. Choose your grade level.
3. Begin your search.

This book's ID number is 9780756540746

FactHound will find the best sites for you.

Index

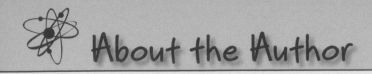

Gina Dal Fuoco

Gina Dal Fuoco has been a teacher for 12 years. She was born and raised near the California coast. Living near the ocean helped develop her curiosity about all the various species that live underwater. She enjoys learning about these creatures while living in California with her husband and two children.

Image Credits